Find the Bathrooms First!

STARTING YOUR NEW JOB ON THE RIGHT FOOT

Roy J. Blitzer
and
Jacquie Reynolds-Rush

D0068364

CRISP PUBLICATIONS

Find the Bathrooms First!

Roy Blitzer and Jacquie Reynolds-Rush

CREDITS:
Editor: George Young, Barbara Artmore
Design and Production: Fifth Street Design, Berkeley, CA

© 1999 Crisp Publications, Inc., Menlo Park, CA 94025

Printed in the United States of America by VonHoffmann Graphics.

http:/www.crisplearning.com

Distribution to the U.S. Trade:
National Book Network, Inc.
4720 Boston Way
Lanham, MD 20706
1-800-462-6420

99 00 01 02 03   10 9 8 7 6 5 4 3 2 1

Library of Congress Card Number 99-75056
Blitzer, Roy J. and Reynolds-Rush, Jacquie
ISBN 1-56052-553-3

CONTENTS

INTRODUCTION

Starting a new job is always a new beginning. It marks a significant change, whether it is a long-awaited promotion, a lateral move to another organization, or a completely different career. Whatever your reason for embarking on a new job, the experience will have its joys and its challenges.

This book is about leveraging the joys and dealing with the challenges. It is about honoring the reasons you made your job choice and creatively assessing the reality of that choice. You put a lot of work, thought, and emotion into finding and landing this new position. Don't stop now. After all your efforts, you have a vested interest in making the next step—your job transition—successful and comfortable.

The focus of this book is about taking care of yourself in the job transition and on *getting your needs met.* We are often so concerned with impressing our new employer that we forget ourselves. As it turns out, meeting your own needs also has the best chance of making you a productive contributor and satisfying your employer. If, after reading this book, you discover that the new job is not meeting your needs, you will understand the reasons why and you will be positioned to take appropriate action.

Most important, you will be in charge of *actively directing your career*—as opposed to being a passive participant responding to the whims of the corporation or marketplace.

This book is divided into three sections. Part One provides information and insight into preparation that's helpful in starting your new position.

Part Two covers your first six weeks on the job. The decisions and assessments you make during this time period are crucial to your career comfort and success. The issues and feelings that surface need to be addressed, attended to and integrated. This section has been divided week by week because these time designations fit the actual time periods that these experiences often take place on the job. It's an easy way to help you focus your thoughts and energy as you go through the transition week by week. Each person's experience, however, will have its own unique time frame and set of circumstances. Therefore, if the week-by-week timing does not suit you, adapt the concepts and timing to your situation.

The final section, Part Three, covers the period in your transition from six weeks to three months. Here you get the opportunity to look at everything from ways to expand your influence and deal with change to validating your commitment and discovering new things about yourself.

As you work through each chapter, you will gain more clarity about whether this job will bring you the level of satisfaction and success that is important to you. You will need to take some time to answer the **Key Questions** for each chapter. You will also want to experiment with some of the **Suggestions for Action**.

In addition, you will be provided with a **Satisfaction Index** which will give you an opportunity to assess what factors are important. You will have tangible criteria upon which to evaluate your observations and gut feelings over time in order to look for the changes and trends.

You will also have a **Transition Journal** available to use to jot down thoughts, ideas and perceptions as you go along day by day. Selected **Key Questions** and **Suggestions for Action** are indicated (*) throughout the book that can be used to help you capture your thoughts and observations for Your Journal.

During the time that we were writing the book, we interviewed people who were going through job transitions. None of these individuals had been in their new positions for more than eight months and many of them were in their first few months. This was not done as formal research, but as a chance for us to touch base in an immediate and focused way. Our interviewees had diverse backgrounds and careers. Included were men and women from their 20's to 60's, with careers in for-profit and non-profit organizations. There were people from small start-up organizations as well people from large well established organizations. These organizations ran the gamut from high-tech to housing, museums to manufacturing, property management to retail, and education to healthcare. Some of our interviewees were switching to a completely new kind of job responsibility and some were entering new market segments. We included individuals who were both single performers and individuals who had supervisory responsibility including senior officer accountability. Jobs included administration, consulting, data networking, employee assistance, finance, human resources, journalism, marketing, sales, software development and technical documentation. We want to express our great appreciation to those people who were willing to talk with us. We found their comments helpful and insightful. In each of the following chapters, you will find quotations taken from these interviews.

This book has been structured so that you can easily choose and select the information that is most helpful to you. This was done so that you can quickly look over the book in total and then use what is most relevant to you and most confortable for your personal style.

By the end of the book, you will have specific data that reflects your best thinking about your situation as you see it. This will help you assess the reality and viability of your career choice and help you create a meaningful plan of action. Good luck!

PART ONE:

·······················

PUTTING <u>YOU</u>
IN THE EQUATION

PREPARING FOR THE JOB

"I'm going to have to create new relationships and figure out how to work with my boss: how we can best communicate and what his work patterns are. I'm starting from square one again." —Mara

From Icon to Inkwell

Everyone moving into a new position feels a sense of excitement and hope. Different opportunities bring with them different people and new challenges. Even if the job is less than your ideal, there are usually some aspects of the job that you are looking forward to. For each person that experience will be different based on his or her own personality, motivations and needs. For the person who has received a promotion or is embarking on a new career there is a special sense of excitement and hope. For the person who had to take a job offer because it was the best available, there may not be the same sense of elation. Still, almost every situation brings something to look forward to and something to learn. Receiving a job offer is a compliment. Allow yourself to fully appreciate and enjoy the feeling of success. Let it give you a sense of renewed energy and enthusiasm.

While changing jobs involves excitement and hope, it also involves loss. We often acknowledge the excitement and hope, and, at the same time, we try to ignore the discomfort. At a minimum, most people in transition have many interwoven emotions and sometimes very mixed feelings. Even when getting a promotion, it's not unusual to still feel sad about what you are leaving. People who can hardly wait to leave their old jobs, are often surprised to find that they feel a sense of loss when they get into the new job. For each individual, the feelings are unique. There are, however, some commonalities. We all have to prove ourselves in our new situation. We often leave behind our status, the trust that we have earned and the relationships that we have built. We depend on these for our sense of community and for our support network. We also leave behind a system and environment that we understand and feel comfortable with. This is especially critical if you're making a transition into a completely different field of endeavor or type of organization.

Some typical transitions are going from:

- An academic environment to a corporate one.
- A nonprofit organization to a for-profit organization and vice versa.
- A large corporation to a small business.
- A rural environment to a city environment and vice versa.
- East Coast to West Coast, or North to South.
- A corporate environment to consulting or consulting to a corporate environment.

The potential in our current economy for dramatic change is great.

With every change, you go from expert back to beginner, from *"Icon to Inkwell"*. The way you deal with the change is significant in how successful your job transition will be.

It is also not unusual when going into any new situation to feel a sense of concern. Just acknowledging these feelings and getting them out in the open can often give you more control. In addition it allows you to think about how you can best deal with your concerns.

This might include:

- Talking about your concerns with your spouse, your partner or a close friend.

- Doing something to bring closure to your prior experience and relationships.

- Thinking about and analyzing how you usually handle transitions to look for repeated patterns.

- Thinking of ways that you can give yourself special support and make things easier.

Talking with someone you care about and who cares about you can really be helpful. It's important to choose someone who is a good listener and will avoid giving you gratuitous advice or trivializing your feelings. The very process of talking with someone who will really listen and who is interested in your welfare gives you a chance to hear yourself think. Suddenly, thoughts and feelings that were not clear before begin to take shape. Someone who has known you for a long time can often bring up behaviors and attitudes that have worked for you in the past. These may be helpful in the new situation. Close friends are often able to empathize. You may find that they have gone through the same thing and have felt the same way. You will probably find that mixed feelings are the rule, not the exception.

Doing something to bring closure to your prior work experience and relationships.

Write a letter, make a call, take people who meant a lot to you out to lunch. Thank those people who reported to you and helped you succeed. Get addresses and phone numbers for those people with whom you will want to stay in contact. Let them know that you want to stay in touch. These things might seem obvious, but sometimes we overlook them in our rush to leave.

Much more difficult to deal with are unresolved differences with former associates. Or the anger you feel because the former organization asked you to leave. Or the discomfort from a misunderstanding you had with someone that you could not clear up. Try to figure out a way to resolve these kinds of issues. Sometimes you can do this by writing a letter. You may want to meet with individuals or call them on the phone to resolve any open issues. If you don't feel that making contact with the individuals involved is appropriate, it often helps just to talk about the situation with someone close to you. Sometimes it also helps just to write down what you would like to say just to get it out of your mind. Once you've gotten these thoughts or feelings resolved, you can leave them behind you. That can be a big advantage. Bringing unresolved problems or negative feelings with you into a job can be very destructive for you personally and certainly for your career.

Thinking about and analyzing how you have handled transitions in the past

Many of us repeat the way that we handle change and thus we often repeat the way that we handle transitions. If you look back at the feelings that you have gone through in past transitions, you will probably find that you have a similar set of feelings now. You know that you've seen all this before and that the mixed emotions are to be expected. This often allows you to be much more understanding about what you are feeling. On the other hand if you are reacting very differently than you usually do, it would make sense to try to understand why.

Giving yourself special support and making things easier

People often make life more difficult for themselves during a transition than they need to. Remember that there are many options. Don't take the most difficult ones. For example, it may be difficult to find the right apartment or buy a home at the same time that you start a job. Sometimes it's much easier to take a short term furnished rental and make the move in a few months. When moving from one city to another, there are many options. For some people having their families or partners with them is the most important consideration. Others would prefer to spend the first couple of weeks or months on the job alone in the new location. This allows them to put tremendous effort into work with no distractions and it does not uproot their family until they have more time to ease the transition.

There are even options in the way you accept the job. It is not uncommon now for individuals to accept jobs on a contract-to-hire or temporary-to-permanent basis. This allows for family members to stay in place until they know the new situation will work. It also allows an opportunity to see if this is the right job. If it isn't, it doesn't have to go on a resume. All involved are free to move on.

Whatever way you go about moving into a new job, make sure that you've given yourself the opportunity to make the transition as easy on yourself and those around you as you can.

KEY QUESTIONS

PREPARING FOR THE JOB

1. What did you like in your old job that you want most to recreate in your new job?

2. What are you happy to let go of from your last job?

3. Have you done everything you need to say goodbye to your old job? If not, what would help you close that chapter of your life?

4. Who do you most want support from in this transition and how can you get it?

5. Who, beside yourself, do you have to think of in this transition?

6. What are the ways that you can make the transition most comfortable for yourself?

7. What are you most looking forward to in the new job?

8. What are three major emotions that describe your feelings about the new position?

9. What advantages exist for you in this new situation both professionally and personally?

Q.1
① Lack of bureaucracy
② Fast decisions
③ Autonomy
④ Ownership
⑤ Flexibility

Q2
① Lack of resources
② Inexperienced managers
③ Sloppy practices

Q7
① Exactly what I want to do
② Strong, growing, resourced, committed org.
③ Doing something worthwhile

Q8
① Awe, excitement, enthusiasm

6 Q9
① Security
② Chance to be major player in ecommerce

Find the Bathrooms First!

SUGGESTIONS FOR ACTION

PREPARING FOR THE JOB

- Give yourself permission to acknowledge a range of emotions and feelings. Talk about them with friends.

- Look over work that you have done previously or performance reviews that you are proud of. This can be a way of remembering and saying goodbye as well as building confidence.

- Treat yourself to something that you especially enjoy.

- Think of at least three ways that you can make life easier for yourself during this transition.

- If your family is going to be impacted by the change, involve them in generating ways to make the change easier.

- If you are moving your family to a new location, ask each family member what one thing he or she wants most at the new location. Try to meet these needs for them.

- Give yourself a pat on the back for taking this new leap of faith!

"The job just isn't a separate category in your life. You're learning about yourself all the time. Knowing yourself is an ongoing activity. It includes when you're at work as well as when you're not."
—Maureen

Knowing Yourself

One major aspect of making a comfortable transition into a new job is understanding yourself. Knowing yourself includes understanding your own feelings and needs. It involves understanding your own values and which values you simply will not compromise. It requires realistically evaluating your abilities and how you can best use them. Knowing yourself also involves clearly acknowledging your expectations about the job.

Knowing Your Values

"I like a direct environment and I can survive in a tough culture. I prefer to be told directly when I'm doing something wrong. I like that kind of culture."—Steve

Values are very basic and vital to each individual. A value is a princi-
ple, quality or situation that has specific reward or meaning for you.
Values that relate to work might include freedom, creativity, variety,
risk, harmony, integrity, personal growth, solid relationships and challenge. Knowing your own values is very important to job satisfaction.
Values are very personal and they are one of the many reasons that
only you can make a decision about whether a job is right for you.
It's unusual to find all your values in one workplace, so it is helpful to
arrange them in order of priority. This helps you decide which values
you simply must have and which you can live without.

Realistically Evaluating your Abilities

Many of us tend to paint our talents and our expectations with a
totally positive brush. Others do just the opposite, and take a heavy
negative focus. From an employer's perspective, every person is a

Does M-M have "values?"
Mine are "spplied" plus fun, flexible, and fast

Find the Bathrooms First!

package of both strengths and weaknesses. You can bet that the people hiring you are looking at both your upside and downside qualities, so it is better that you think along the same lines.

Be sure that you give yourself credit for all your abilities. Most of us understand the more tangible ones that we have, but don't give ourselves credit for abilities like determination, tenacity or getting along well with people. It's also necessary to distinguish between those we have and those we are willing to use at work. For example you may be excellent at math and great at detail, but may prefer not to use those capabilities on the job. Some people choose to compartmentalize their lives including their capabilities and others think of work and life as one continuum. Where do you stand?

Think through how your abilities match the challenge of the job. What is special about you? What will you bring to this job that few other people can bring? If you are a person who can literally see yourself in the job, what do you see yourself doing? If visioning doesn't work for you, just think about yourself on the job. What is exciting about it? What's important? Unfortunately, many of us are socialized to think certain attributes in a job are what we should want. When it comes right down to it, those may not be the attributes that are really important to us.

As a balance, it's also important to think about any difficulties you might have related to this job. Looking at old performance reviews and focusing on areas for improvement can help you do this.

Reflection on your interview can also help. Sometimes during an interview, the interviewer will bring up reservations or concerns. These reservations may be completely off the mark or they may be an accurate appraisal of your capabilities. In either case, they should be considered important information. You will need to approach your job in a way that will put these concerns to rest. There is often an assumption that, if you are offered a position, concerns no longer exist. More often the reality is that you are offered the job despite the concerns.

Perhaps, unrelated to any other outside factor, you, yourself, are concerned about your ability to carry out some aspect of the job. This can be because it is a new type of job responsibility, it includes something you don't like doing, or it involves some area where you have limited capability. This can be reason for concern, but also an opportunity for growth.

People who are most successful are those who figure out not only how to leverage their talents and abilities, but also how to minimize their shortcomings. It's important to realize that everyone has them. Those people who succeed learn how to manage their limitations so they don't get in their way. Chances are that in the past, you have consciously or unconsciously done just that.

Acknowledging and Managing Your Expectations

Everyone has a set of expectations about a new job. These expectations may include what you can contribute, what you think your supervisor will be like and judgments about the work environment. If you can make these expectations clear to yourself, you will be able to use them. They will help you evaluate your new environment quickly. If you don't take the time to clarify your own expectations, issues may arise that you will be unable to define, act on or confront.

A first step in building a sound basis for your expectations is understanding why you chose the job. This involves such factors as:

- ✓ compensation
- ✓ scope of influence
- ✓ the kind of work environment
- opportunity for advancement
- ✓ opportunity for learning
- chance to be a supervisor
- chance to be an individual performer

✓• opportunity to do work you love

✓• opportunity to accomplish something important

• demonstrated shared values

The reasons you chose the job are as multifaceted as you are. Thinking through these reasons and putting them in priority can help you to better understand your expectations.

Step two in clarifying expectations in your new position is to distinguish between what you want to accomplish for yourself and what you want to accomplish for the organization. Hopefully the two will be congruent. If they aren't, spend some time thinking about how you can make them come together. For example, someone might choose a job as a public relations specialist in a theater arts company because he wants to learn more about theater. How can he do the public relations work necessary to the organization and still get involved in aspects of the theatre he wants to learn more about?

The last major component of forming realistic expectations is getting a handle on why you were selected for the job. How does this fit with how you perceive yourself? We are usually both so relieved and so pleased when we get a job offer, we don't stop to wonder or ask what went into our selection. Sometimes we're told during the job offer, although the actual reason can be somewhat different or more complex.

" I was brought in because my experience was a fit. I could bring them from a transactions business to a solutions and applications business" —Greg W

"They volunteered that they were interested in a couple of things . . . management experience, engineering experience and leadership " —Kay

Usually it is fairly easy to figure out the traditional skills that you were hired for. It is more difficult is to figure out some of the reasons that are not so straightforward. The reason people are hired, besides their basic skills, are many and incredibly varied. Here is a list of just a few.

- You're like the last person in the job.

- You're completely different from the last person in the job.

- You have some personality traits that are needed in the department, group or project.

- You're perceived as a leader.

- You're perceived as someone who won't rock the boat.

- You're perceived as someone who will add status.

- You have a contact or networking base that can bring in business.

- Someone in a position of power liked you.

- People in the group feel you're not a threat.

This list could go on for pages and you could probably add reams to it from your past experience.

Think through the interview process. Think about not only what was said, but also what you observed about the company. Talk with those people who were your references. What they said about you helped to set the organization's rationale for hiring you. Sometimes the individual doing the referencing may have shared some of the thinking of the organization with your reference.

Using any clues or information acquired, now is the time to come up with the most informed expectation you can. Know that this expectation will have to be expanded and revised as you integrate into the organization. Be prepared to approach this as an open question. Only time will tell you what the reality is.

With your values, abilities and expectations in mind, you now have a compass to help chart your new direction accurately. This does not mean that you can't revise or change your assessment, as you become more familiar with the job. It does mean that, even before starting the job, you are taking conscious control of the process that will define your job experience.

KEY QUESTIONS

KNOWING YOURSELF

1. What are your reasons for choosing the job?*

2. Why do you think you were selected for the job?

3. How will you use your strengths in this job?

4. How will you manage your downsides in this job?

5. If you got any feedback from the last job, how can it help you in the new job?

6. How do you think your new employer perceives you?

7. What do you hope most to accomplish for the organization in this new job?*

8. What values are absolutely critical for you in a job?*

9. What do you hope most to accomplish for yourself?*

Q1
① Compensation
② Security
③ Type of work I want

Q2
① Perfect fit

SUGGESTIONS FOR ACTION

KNOWING YOURSELF

- Write down the two most important values that you must find in your workplace in order to be successful.* (Refer to #8 in Key Question section above.)

- Write down the two most important values that you must find in your workplace in order to respect others that you work with? *

- Write down your top three reasons for choosing this job.*

- Give thought to the interviews you went through. Write down your insights into what influenced your selection for the job?*

- If any concerns or reservations were mentioned during the hiring process, plan how you can most effectively overcome them.

- Call to thank your references and let them know about your new job. Ask them for any information they might have picked up.

- Look over work that you have done previously or past performance reviews. Think through how this information can be helpful to you in the new position.

- Think about how you've managed your downsides in the past and how you can apply that to the future.

"I want balance . . . I spend time with my wife and family. I talk to a confidante I have in LA. I'm also careful with my health and am in a good exercise program." —Jules

"I have seven children and I'm their sole support. I don't get into what about me stuff. If I need someone to listen; I talk to my husband or go out with him." —Genetha

Your *Transition Journal*

A new position represents a major life transition and change. It requires a lot of energy. We all respond differently to new situations, experiences and stress. Some people use exercise. Others talk things out, sharing their thoughts and experiences with people they can relate to. Others read, write poetry, paint or do woodworking. Still others "chat" with support groups on the Internet. Many do several of the above and more.

The purpose of the **Transition journal** is to keep track of your thoughts, emotions and feelings as they occur—to log on a regular basis what is going on in your work life. It's a way to capture what's happening to you and to pinpoint the experiences in real time. The benefits are substantial:

- You can learn from what you write.

- You can make better decisions.

- You can "let go" of what's bothersome or annoying.

- You can track your progress.

- You can see what's important to you.

- You can get things "off your chest" and unload.

- You can be creative and imaginative.

People in the helping professions have been recommending "journalizing" for years, (Ira Progoff pioneered the *Intensive Journal Technique* as a way to help people work out some problems). It's a proven way to deal with feelings, thoughts and activities. Many people see events differently and from a new perspective after they come back and re-read their entries.

Another reason for keeping a transitional journal is to chart the evolution of your thinking. Do you still have some of the same questions after three months that you had in the first week? If issues existed, have they been resolved, and how? Perhaps you were delighted your first two weeks, but you are not as happy now. What's happened? This kind of record can help you make a much more informed analysis to chart your future direction.

A transitional journal is also a good place to jot down any creative approaches that you may think about, resolutions to work problems or new ideas for future projects. When you are new in a company, you have a fresh perspective. You often have many ideas that cannot be achieved immediately. If you write them down, however, they are always there for you to use in the future.

It is also possible to use the entire record as a summary of events. If you keep a transition journal, you will be able to learn a great deal about yourself and transitions. This is helpful information for what you are going through in the present and will also be helpful to you in the future. If you develop a pattern of keeping a journal during work transitions, you will be able to pick out patterns of how you personally make transitions. You will begin to see what works for you and what doesn't. You'll know what's easier for you and what's more difficult. Having this knowledge will help you better prepare for transitions in the future.

Keep your journal in any way that most appeals to you. *Keep it in any way that will help you actually make it happen.* It really doesn't matter what format you choose—bound notebook, 3 x 5 cards, organizer pages, special confidential computer file. It just needs to be comfortable for you to access and easy to get into.

Set your own guidelines and heed them. Regularity and consistency are the keys. Some ideas that might work include:

- Dating your daily entries.

- Writing at the same time (i.e. before bed, early morning etc).

- Using ink (pencil will eventually fade over the years).

- Not worrying about spelling, grammar and syntax.

- Capturing immediate thoughts.

- Using stream of consciousness.

Keep in mind that this journal is just for you. It is not a document that anyone else will ever need to read. Do and say whatever pleases you and gives you information.

KEY QUESTIONS

YOUR TRANSITION JOURNAL

Asterisks (*) have been placed by some Key Questions and Suggestion For Action throughout the book. These are used to designate especially helpful things to include in your Transition Journal. Use them or any others in the book, as you feel appropriate.

SUGGESTIONS FOR ACTION

YOUR TRANSITION JOURNAL

- List key processes or relationships that you observe on the job.

- Jot down your key co-workers or customers. Describe impressions or reactions.
  E.g., Sally - Admin, at front of area. Met first thing. Went out of her way to be helpful. 1/16/99 — Day One.

- Try poetry as a way to express your feelings.

- Write something every day—an idea, a reaction, an emotion. Write something, anything!

- Keep track of action items, people to contact, perceptions and conversations you want to have.

- Leave space for answers to **Key Questions** you choose to answer or **Suggestions for Action you want to use later.**

- Draw a picture or diagram of what you've put down in words.

"On the first job I ever had, I had a phenomenal first day. From the time I arrived, they treated me like an honored guest. That's the first and last time that happened to me." —Greg R

"This may seem like a small thing, but I honestly feel that someone ought to be charged with taking you to lunch the first day and acquainting you with what's around there. So you won't be groping around for where to eat and someone to talk to. However it's never happened to me." —Carol G

"That first day was disorganized. They were not ready for me though they knew I was coming—-no office, nowhere to sit, nowhere to put things." —Genetha

The First Day

The First Day on any job leaves lasting memories. While interviewing people about their experiences in the first few months at work, it became apparent that the first day of any new job leaves lasting memories for almost everyone. Some people experienced outstanding first days. This left them with good feelings about the organization and a tremendous desire to be a contributing member of the group. The majority of the people had experienced first days that were far from positive. Let's just say that most organizations would not like a rendition to appear in their recruiting brochures. In fact it seems a paradox to put so much time, effort and money into recruiting employees and then to so often completely ignore them once they arrive on the job.

The reality seems to be that for many, first days are disappointing at best and demeaning at worst.

"If I had had a heart attack in the newsroom, I thought my colleagues might have covered it as a news story, but they wouldn't have dialed 911. After six hours, I realized that this was not the place for me." —Carol B

"Emotionally it's like being the new kid in school. You don't know anybody, you don't know your way around. Everybody else is just fine and nobody is concerned about integrating you. It feels like when you were a kid and nobody wanted to play with you." —Carol G

A Dialogue to Help Think Things Through — Roy Blitzer and Jacquie Reynolds-Rush

JRR: Roy, it seems to me that from our interviews the first day of work often sets the tone for the early part of the transition, and sometimes the experience affects people's feelings about the organization for months.

RJB: Day One basically is a key day. The most important purpose should be to build confidence. Best case, it builds self-confidence; confidence in the organization and confidence in your new supervisor.

JRR: It is not unusual for people to arrive at the workplace and find that their supervisor is not there, they have no desk, telephone or workspace, and in fact no one expected them. In some instances the individual has trouble getting through security.

RJB: Needless to say, besides being very deflating and disappointing, that certainly does not build confidence in the organization. It also does nothing for your own self-confidence.

JRR: Exactly. So the question is how can you prepare for the day emotionally, mentally and physically so that you're up for whatever happens?

RJB: A lot has to do with your own personality. It's important to honor who you are. With some thought and planning you can build in ways to make the day easier.

JRR: It's also helpful to make no assumptions. Be open to whatever the day may bring.

RJB: The day, of course, begins long before getting to work. It helps to give yourself enough time to feel relaxed. Getting up thirty minutes to an hour before you usually start getting ready for work can save a lot of aggravation.

JRR: Think about ways that you can make life easier for yourself. Start with the preparation for the day. Wear something that fits in with the dress code of the organization, but also make it something you like that is comfortable. Eat what you love most for breakfast. Leave a lot of additional time for any traffic or commute issues. If you have children, plan for a trusted support system to back you up, so that you minimize obstacles to your peace of mind.

RJB: Let's assume that by giving yourself extra time and arranging your mornings before work for maximum comfort, you'll put yourself in the best space to face the day. The best way to be prepared for the day at work is to think through a best-case scenario and a worst-case scenario. Be prepared for both and anything in between.

JRR: Jobs often start on Monday morning when people are trying to shift from the weekend activities and trying to just get their heads together.

RJB: It can save you a lot of uncomfortable moments to get information beforehand about what the starting time really means. If you are told that starting time is 8:00, is that the time people really start, or do they actually start about 9:00.

JRR: One way to create a good start to the day is to set up a meeting with your supervisor for the specific time you are to arrive. Arrange the meeting by phone several days before your first day. This is helpful in several ways. It's a reminder that you're coming and perhaps will initiate some preparation for your arrival. It also brings you up to date with what may have happened in the organization since you last talked.

When is starting time?
Where is my office?
Process for selecting
secretary?

Find the Bathrooms First!

RJB: That would be a best-case scenario, but of course even with that kind of planning anything can happen.

JRR: Absolutely. You could still get to work and find that your supervisor is sick, late or has been transferred or terminated, and that no one is expecting you. That would be a worst-case scenario.

RJB: So, being prepared for the worst-case scenario, you want to have your employment letter with you as well as any information you may need to fill out new-hire paperwork. It helps to have identification and personal data.

JRR: One person I interviewed said she brings a briefcase with Post-Its, highlighter, pencils, pens, paper and everything else she thinks she might have to use that day. If she can't get her hands on supplies right away, she's prepared.

RJB: You mean she brings her own supply case! Great, I like that, and, I guess it also goes without saying that you should have your calendar or personal organizer with you so that you can begin to set up meetings, appointments, timetables etc.

JRR: Definitely. Also bring a cell phone if you have one. It's not unusual to find no phone service at your desk. Maybe, for that matter, no desk or workspace either. It's also a good idea to bring something productive to work on. Bring information to read about the organization or technical articles related to the work you'll be doing. In case circumstances make it difficult for you to become immediately involved, you have something to do that is of benefit to the company.

RJB: We've talked a lot about the situation where you walk in and essentially have to create the workday for yourself. On the other hand, there is also the situation where you walk in and you're immediately swept into the eye of the storm. Long overdue work has been left for you, or an emergency has come about or a meeting has been organized that involves you immediately.

For Steve - like to listen first.
say 3 - 4 weeks
Anything I can add value to immediately?
Short-term/long-term goals

JRR: That's unusual and that calls for a ready-for-anything-attitude. Sometimes you walk into a first day that has been so over-planned that you don't have time to catch your breath. You feel like a marathon runner.

RJB: People want to know your opinions. How you might change things. How you will approach problems.

JRR: I've seen so many people get in trouble in those situations. Outside of having to solve an emergency problem threatening the organization or threatening life and limb, it's really important to hold back for a few weeks until you're beginning to under-stand the organization and the culture. It's really OK to be clear that you're new and you want to fully understand the issues before you jump in with opinions and suggestions. Give your-self a chance to understand the situation. People will usually respect your efforts to get to know the organization first before making judgments.

RJB: If you have a forceful personality that's going to be hard to do. That's a big challenge.

JRR: True, but it's so much better than coming up with solutions or processes that have to be abandoned a month later or that are apparent to all as rash misjudgments. On the other hand, if you have knowledge that can complete a project or a process that is straightforward and much needed — go for it. Certainly that quickly conveys the perception that you'll be a real contributor.

RJB: So, before we sign off, let's quickly go over some of the "do's and don'ts" that will help towards a better first day. Some even might need to be done ahead of time.

JRR: **Do** try to set up the day as much as possible before you get there. If you can negotiate for the kind of workspace you are going to have with the offer, do so. If possible the week before you start, set up some appointments with your supervisor and co-workers for your first day.

RJB: **Do** bring a cell phone, if you have one. Be prepared to call the switchboard when you arrive to let the people taking incoming calls know you're there. If you have not been given a desk or phone yet, give them your cell phone number. Organize your life so you won't have to be getting a lot of outside calls your first day.

JRR: **Do** have flexible plans for lunch so that if you're asked to lunch you can go. If you aren't, do something that's a real support and treat. If you know the area, plan to go to a nearby restaurant that you love or find relaxing. You may find it ideal to pack a lunch and escape to the park or the car to relax. Some people may feel really comfortable finding the cafeteria and discovering what's there. The important point is to think ahead about what's most emotionally pleasing to you.

RJB: **Do** ask for organization charts, phone books or department personnel lists before you get there so you can bring those with you and refresh your memory about people you've met. Many places now don't like to use organization charts and phone lists. Hopefully you've kept the business cards that you got while interviewing. Use them to review names and numbers. Start a beginning phone list for yourself.

Tom
Tim
Dick
Laura
Sandy
Chuck?

JRR: **Do** bring something with you that will make you feel at home in your new workspace. For some people it's pictures, for others it's books or magazines, and for others it may be things like a candy dish with candy or handmade ceramic pencil holder. Bring what's easy to transport and what will work even where your arrangements may be temporary. What's important is that it makes the space feel like yours. It also serves the purpose of sending nonverbal messages about who you are to your co-workers. It makes a statement about you.

RJB: **Do** keep plans flexible for the evening after your first day. Be prepared to stay beyond the normal end-of-workday schedule, if necessary. Schedule something that you enjoy. You may just want to go home and go to bed or read a good book. Keep your calendar clear of commitments. Limit outside commitments during the time you're starting a new job.

JRR: To sum up, the key to the best first day possible is to be prepared for any contingency. If you expect nothing, it's not such a shock or disappointment if that's what you get. If, on the other hand, the organization is prepared to welcome you, what a nice surprise!

RJB: Exactly, and it's also important not to jump to conclusions about the company based on your first-day experience. That can leave you a lot of emotions that are not helpful to a comfortable and successful transition.

"To survive the first day, you need to have yourself pretty together!"
—Carol G

Part Two:

THE FIRST SIX WEEKS

"I try to do a lot of listening initially; I'm a sponge. I listen to every-thing anyone wants to tell me. You are certainly never going to learn anything by being a talker." —Carol G

WEEK ONE

Who are These People?

Let's assume for a moment that you are at home watching a movie on TV. Instead of a remote control, you have an on-site control that allows you to step into the action on the screen. If you could do that, you would find that the characters are vastly more multidimensional than you perceived from watching them. You would also find yourself interacting differently with the char-acters if you joined them during a train wreck than if you joined them during an elegant dinner party.

Your first week at work is just such an experience. Essentially you step into your "pre-hire picture." For most of us that pre-hire picture is very strong and compelling. After all, our decision to join the organization was based on observations during the hiring process. We are always quite invested in those observations and decisions that led us to commit to the job.

Nevertheless, it is very important for our survival and our peace of mind to see people and events in full perspective. This is particularly important in today's work environment, where often the picture changes dramatically from the time you are hired to the time you start the job. Between the time you are interviewed and the day you start your new job, it is not unusual for supervisors to change, work groups to change, and major reorganizations to take place.

The most important objective for the first week is to understand your work environment and the people in it. You will also want to help them get to know and understand who you are. Through this process, you will begin to work on the basic building block of success: trust.

> *"The moment I came into the place, it felt wonderful. There was such energy and spirit"* —Maureen

Immediately, you will need to begin to assess what kind of environment you're stepping into and the many dimensions of the key characters who are important to your work. Have you joined a group that's managing a disaster, putting out fires, truly working at a high level or cruising along with business as usual? Once you begin to understand the issues impacting this group, you will begin to acquire the information necessary to give yourself the most comfortable and effective introduction. You will understand what you can give to the group that they most need.

At the same time that you are assessing the environment of your new work group, you also need to focus on the key individuals who will be important to you. Some of the most important information you need to know about your supervisor and co-workers includes:

- How can you be most helpful to them?
- What is the best time to get their attention?
- How do they think?
- What is the prevailing leadership style?
- What is their communication style?
- How do they manage conflict?

If you assess the environment and the people in a balanced way, you will be able to understand the group more accurately. As you move into the group, you will be able to integrate in a way that helps support the group and at the same time allows you to measure how this situation meets your needs.

No one expects you to save the company the first week you are there. Introduce yourself to the group in a low-key manner. You don't need to be a hero or a superwoman. Your co-workers want to feel that you're someone they can work with and trust. That should be your agenda too. Find out. Can you work with and trust these people? Look for people who:

- Will give you valid information.
- Are candid and forthcoming.
- Stop to explain things to you.
- Give you balanced information and feedback.
- Don't try to recruit you to any cause or perspective.

At the end of the first week, you should have a baseline for the individuals important to your work and some feeling for how you can work comfortably with them. Once you have this baseline, you will have turned your first week into a comfort zone you can build on over the weeks to come.

KEY QUESTIONS

WEEK ONE

1. How does my function fit into the total success of the operation?

2.* What information about my boss do I most need to know?

3.* What are the things that are most important to my boss?

4.* How can I be helpful to my boss immediately?

5.* How does my boss manage the group?

6.* Are the leaders in my group/department/team competent? If not, how does the group manage them?

7. Is the group in a crisis mode or does the environment seem stable?

8. How does the work group most effectively communicate with each other?

9. What have been the most effective times of day to communicate with individuals in the group?

10. How does my boss like information to be presented?

*11. How often does my boss want to be informed? Are there other people to keep informed?

12. How does each co-worker give information — in large concepts or small details?

13.* What are the individual preferences for types of communication, (e-mail, voice-mail, phone conversation, in person)?

14.* Is there an "open-door policy"—If not, what's the acceptable process for dealing with closed doors if I need to get someone's attention?

15. What is considered an emergency and who do I need to notify if such an event happens?

16. How does my boss handle conflict?

17. How do key people in the group handle conflict?

18. How can the people around me be most helpful to me in understanding or accomplishing my job?

19. What has been my most significant insight or realization this week about my job/situation? *

SUGGESTIONS FOR ACTION

WEEK ONE

- Share your enthusiasm about joining the group.

- Choose what you think is important to let people know about you and share it openly. Self-disclosure implies warmth and trust.

- Don't be hesitant to actively ask for help and support. Get the information you need.

- Acknowledge, recognize and thank those individuals who help you.

- Telegraph to others that they are important by giving them adequate time and your complete attention.

- Establish yourself as a good listener. Let your co-workers do most of the talking.

- Keep your commitments and don't make any promises you can't keep. Follow up, as agreed, on all conversations and work in progress.

- Learn as much as you can about people in your work group. Ask for a description of a recent problem and its solution. Listen for word cues that tell you how they think.

- Arrive at work slightly earlier than your work group and stay slightly later. Do this for the first six weeks.

- Talk with your supervisor at least three different times during the week. Select different times of day for each meeting. See which times he/she is more receptive and relaxed.*

- Sit down with at least three key people in your work group and ask them how you can be most helpful in working with them.

- Be attentive and helpful to those around you whenever you have the chance. Demonstrate that you are a team player.

Find the Bathrooms First!

- Ensure that you keep sensitive information confidential. If you are not sure what is sensitive, err on the side of caution.

- Receive negative information about the company with an open mind. Do not ignore it or embrace it. See if the information fits, as you go through the next few weeks.

"My daughter told me that I choose my jobs like I do my husbands. She says I only look at the positives and never look at the flaws."
—Maureen

WEEK TWO

Hope Meets Reality

We all go into each new job, each new challenge, with some sense of hope. The blueprint for hope is unique to each individual, much like our individual fingerprint. Success and satisfaction are made up of many different components. You need to know what's important to you. Hope can range from what we want our work group to be like, to how we want to serve our customers. It can be specific, such as hoping to be promoted in six months, or broad, such as hoping that you can feel pride in the mission of the organization. We may hope that our new job will allow us to gain new skills, influence a wider group of people, give us more time with our family or perhaps a combination of all three. If our hopes are not in some way realized, it is impossible for us to commit to any job or any challenge.

At the same time that we cling to our hopes, the individuals in our workplace also have hopes. They have hopes for themselves and for you, the new hire. They may hope that you are an expert and will be able to bring your expertise to the day-to-day tasks. They may view you as the person who will best fit into a closely knit team. On the other hand, they may have selected you because they view you as very different and hope that you will bring a different dimension to their effort.

In order to begin to grapple with hope realistically and to put it in a context, it is helpful to look at the following:

- The values of the organization

- The mission of the company

- The relationship between management's actions and words

- The content of your work

In your investigations, you will be taking a pragmatic look at your situation. It is important to test the waters and find out what is truly realistic both from your perspective and from your employer's perspective. Now is the time to distinguish between "realistic hope" (that which is *likely to happen*) and "hope against hope" (that which has little chance of fulfillment).

The Values of the Organization

> "The difference between what I expected and the reality was fore-most the culture. There was much more intensity and confrontation. In some environments you can say "I don't know," but not in the one I'm in." —Steve

Values are the bedrock of the organization. You begin to feel them immediately, even if you don't identify them consciously. It can be very helpful, however, to consciously identify them as soon as possible. They are your guideposts to what the organization expects from you.

Earlier, you had the opportunity to think about and identify your most important values. Now you need observe the values of the organization in operation. This is important both for your ability to function effectively and also to determine if your values fit with the values of the organization well enough for you to be committed to the organization.

One reason that people instantly feel comfortable in an organization is that their values match those of the organization. On the other hand, one of the most frequent reasons that "good jobs go bad" is that once an individual gets into a job, he or she finds that the values in the organization are really quite different than they had anticipated. Most often this is not because people in the organization have been disingenuous, it's because communicating about values is so difficult. We generally use broad descriptive words, which can mean many different things. People within an organization begin to repeatedly use certain phrases and buzz-words to describe the values in their organization. Within the organization, the meaning of those phrases is mutually understood. A person from outside the company or new to the company may find that they would not describe what they see in the same way.

For example:

- The term "close-knit" may turn out to be a euphemism for "clique."

- The term "aggressive" may turn out to be a euphemism for attacking.

- The term "upbeat" or "positive" may turn out to mean that conflict is not allowed to surface.

- The term "teamwork" may turn out to mean that there is no personal responsibility for results.

Sometimes the reason that we are not clear about the values of the organization is that there is often a tendency to screen out what we don't want to see or hear during the interview process. Our observations or assessment can be clouded by what we wish to see, or what is being offered.

Since discussions and pre-hire observations reflecting values can be so imprecise, one often is in for a surprise. Therefore it helps to go into an organization with an open mind to observe what happens on a daily basis.

A major clue about the values of an organization is how people spend their time. In some organizations, people spend a large percentage of their time relating with each other. In some, relating to others is a low priority; most of the time is spent in accomplishing the job solo. There are organizations where putting in extensive overtime is considered not "working smart." In others, people work until late into the evening, whether they need to or not. It's considered a demonstration of commitment; it means you're a hard worker and really care. There are the organizations where people are always meeting behind closed doors. In other organizations managers are seldom in their offices, but out where the work is happening. There are the organizations where people spend a tremendous amount of "face time" with senior management. In some organizations people meet on short notice. In others, time is prescheduled very rigidly. These are only a few of the ways people spend time in organizations. Each organization has its own time profile. As you understand how people spend time, you will have a vital clue about what's important to people in the organization.

Another way to judge values is what people talk about and how they talk about it. Do they talk a lot about the customer or are they focused on internal issues? When they evaluate each other's work, do they do it constructively, or do they tear it apart? In some organizations people say what they mean directly. In others, you hear a lot of conversation before they get to the point.

Who people admire is another indication of values. As people discuss work that has taken place, events that have occurred and where to turn to for answers, it becomes clear who they admire. These may be formal or informal leaders. To understand the values in an organization, it is very important to know who these people are and to understand why they are admired.

As you assess the values in your organization, consider how these values fit for you. If you are feeling good about the organization, the chances are that your values and the organization's are a good match. If you are feeling vaguely uncomfortable, it's important to spend enough time to contrast your values with what you are observing in the organization. As you do this, it is often possible to connect your values with those in the organization even if they don't start out as a fit in the beginning.

The Mission

"I really wanted to work for them because of their mission. They carried out their mission in very creative ways." —Mara

Many organizations have a mission statement. If there is a mission statement, it's important to read it and understand what it means to those in the organization. Think about the reality of the statement to what you are observing on an everyday basis. Is the mission obvious in the work you see going on, or is it irrelevant? Where the mission statement is accurate, it will be used often on a working level. You will hear people refer to it. It may be used to evaluate results and direction. People will have copies and keep them handy. If the mission statement is irrelevant, it will be used only as rhetoric.

Relationship Between Management's Actions and Words.

"Over the years I've observed that when companies talk a lot about having an open-door policy, it always means that they don't. In companies where they really do have an open-door policy, they don't do a lot of talking about it. The managers just make themselves available when you need to see them." —Carol G

You will very quickly be able to notice whether management's words and actions are congruent. Certainly the most striking example is how closely the situation you're now in matches what you were told when you were interviewed. If what you were told is not consistent with how things really are, it's important to understand why. Reasons for this type of inconsistency can run the gamut from a change in senior management or business direction to plain misrepresentation. If things are not consistent with what you were told, it's important to understand why. You then have a better chance to handle the situation in a way that includes your best interests. Your first weeks provide the perfect time to observe how the words and actions of the managers relate. It is at this time that you can be a most unbiased observer, before you become accustomed to how things are. If the words and actions that you observe don't seem congruent, use the actions as your guide.

The Content of Your Work

> *"In my past jobs there was a clear understanding more or less what the responsibilities were and what the roles were. There was always a little crossing of the lines, based on the personalities involved. But in this organization, it's anything you can do to get a customer. That becomes your business plan."* —Greg R

In an ideal world, you will be able to get a real grasp on the content of your work by the second week you are on the job. If a formal job description exists, you should certainly have a copy. Hopefully you have had a meeting with your supervisor, who has given you a list of priorities. You would have talked with some key co-workers who have given you some idea of what they hope you will bring to the job. Certainly you would make a concerted effort to make all these things happen during your first week in the organization.

It is not unusual however, to come in the first week and find that your supervisor is off site for the week, or you have to be off site for the first week with training or an unexpected project. It is also not unusual to find that there is no stated job description. Sometimes when you go into a new position, you are the first person to hold the position. The main responsibility for creating the content of the job is yours, with input and approval from your supervisor.

Whether the job has been very clearly laid out or whether it is very ill defined, it's helpful to create a job description for yourself. It can be as simple as notes to something that is much more structured. The intent is to give you a chance to create a working document based on what you think is necessary and realistic for you to perform the job. This should be a work in progress over the first few months. It's a way for you to organize your thoughts and clarify areas that may not be clear. It's also a way to put the elements of your job.

Use the information to organize and guide your discussions with your supervisor. If you use this as a work in progress, you have a flexible process for including other's thinking, while still maintaining some control over the outcome.

Sometimes you may find that the job you thought you were taking simply doesn't exist. You may be asked to do something completely different. This often is true in small, new organizations where the business situation changes rapidly. It also happens in large organizations where internal structures have changed or where the organizational environment is not adequately prepared. In other words, hiring you was an act of wishful thinking or budget opportunity. You may be asked to do something quite different for a few months based on the organization's need.

These are always disquieting situations, but may also be potentially great opportunities. It may be that you were hired not only for what you know, but also for your perceived ability to learn and be flexible. It's usually worthwhile to take a wait-and-see attitude. It's also important to ask questions and clarify the situation. Do so until you are satisfied that you understand what is going on and why. The more you understand the situation, the better able you will be to make the job you were hired for come together. Be an active participant in the configuration of your job responsibilities and the way they are carried out.

KEY QUESTIONS

WEEK TWO

1. What have you noticed about how the organization manages time? What does it tell you about the values of the organization?*

2. What have you noticed about the values of the organization?

3. When you watch the formal leaders in the group, what values do you see demonstrated?*

4. Who are the informal leaders in the group? What can you learn from them?*

5. Does the organization have a mission statement?

6. How does the organization put the mission into action?

7. If you attended an orientation, how was the organization represented? What kind of format and physical setting was involved?

8. Is your job the same as what you thought you would be doing, when you accepted the job? If not, what's different and why?*

9. Do you feel a sense of comfort with the people that you most need to work with? If not, why? How can you make the relationships more comfortable?

10. What expectations do people seem to have regarding you? Are there any expectations that don't seem realistic?

11. Was there anything negative that you were expecting that hasn't happened. Have your worst fears materialized?*

12. What do your instincts tell you about this job and this organization?*

13. Is the organization's image in the marketplace backed up by what you've observed so far? How?

SUGGESTIONS FOR ACTION

WEEK TWO

- Write down the key values of the organization. Star the top three values.*

- If the values of the organization and your values differ, look for a fit within subgroups in the organization.

- Identify people with similar values as your own. Observe how they are able to function effectively in the organization.*

- Try to find one or two aspects of the job or the organization that will most give you satisfaction in the job. Write them down and amplify them as you learn more about the organization.*

- Make sure that you get a copy of your formal job description, if one exists.

- Create a job description for yourself. Make it a work in progress. If a formal job description exists, use it as a basis for your own.

- If the job is really different than you expected, discuss it with your supervisor to get clarification. Be open to what opportunities may exist in the situation. Build on those opportunities toward what you want.

- Read whatever you can find about the organization: published literature, the products and the services. Include marketing literature, press releases, product and web-site information.

- Try to talk with someone in public relations or community relations to better understand the company image.

WEEK THREE

"I realized that I was not going to be supported by my boss because he didn't have any support or backing by management. That meant there was no way he could stand up for me." —Carol G

"I thought it was strange that people would constantly ask me what kind of mood my boss was in. I finally found out why one day when I heard her walk into someone's office and start screaming." —Maureen

Where are The Skeletons Buried?

Skeletons: Yours and Theirs

Each person brings to the workplace a certain amount of buried treasure and a whole lot of baggage. These are issues, situations and experiences that have not been discussed or fully discussed with the employer. The buried treasure, of course, is a bonus you bring to the organization. Buried treasure is made up of capabilities, experience, information or connections in the marketplace that are not specifically job related, but still relevant to the organization. It will be up to you to bring this bonus to the fore. You may also bring with you life issues and past work experience that could be negatives for the organization. Managing these will be pivotal to your comfort level while at work and to your successful integration into the organization.

The organization, on the other hand, may have issues, situations and practices that also have not been discussed. These may impact your job and your job performance. They may be fairly obvious to you or hidden in the shadows. You may never know what they are. Occasionally, however, the shadow moves away and for a brief moment, you get a glimpse of what's really there. Someone says something. You observe an interaction going on.

You read a memo that seems strange, not consistent with what you know to exist. When that happens, it's like being handed a piece of a puzzle. Don't ignore it, and don't jump to conclusions. Jot down your observations in your transition journal. Over a period of time you may pick up enough clues to figure out the puzzle and find out what's behind the shadow.

Life happens. Each organization is a community with all the same kind of situations that happen in any community. That's a given. Therefore, situations may arise that impact you and your success. Something you did in the past has repercussions. Something someone else says takes on a life of it's own. Something is going on in the organization that you did not anticipate. On rare occasions, these things can be serious. Most often they just make your working situation a little more challenging or awkward. Sometimes you can do something about them, sometimes you can't. If one is even able to simply understand the dynamics of what is taking place, it's a big help. It can save you a lot of grief. Of course, once you are able to understand the situation, you will need to take whatever action seems possible and appropriate.

Given the number of job changes that people currently seem to make, the chances are that most of us will run into one of the skeletons at least once. With that in mind, let's look more closely at some of the skeletons that can exist both for you and the organization.

Skeletons in YOUR Closet

Situations in your life can have a great effect on your work. There may be things that you have not discussed with your employer, but, if you let them, they can come to work with you every day. And they can even affect your performance.

Personal Problems and Responsibilities: Do whatever you can to minimize these when you come to the workplace. It's obvious they don't help your work performance. More important, they bring you a tremendous amount of stress. Get all the support you can from friends and family. Leave as much time as you can between the time you leave home and the time you get to work in order to let any issues defuse. Allow yourself to let your work be a pleasant distraction from your personal issues or problems. If you have children, set clear parameters around when they can call you and for what reasons. If childcare is involved, make every effort to organize your childcare so that you will feel totally comfortable at work. If you are going through a short term but demanding personal commitment or issue like the birth of a baby, the death of a family member, problems with your childcare, personal or family illness, let your supervisor know. Work together to find a way that things can be handled.

Burnout: In our rapid-paced workplace, burnout can often be nipping at your heels. Unfortunately, it's not uncommon to bring burnout with you from your old job into your new position. This is a tough situation to handle. A big step in the right direction is to at least identify what is happening. Knowing that this is really related to your old position and not your new one can be very helpful. Evidence of burnout includes unfinished projects, missing deadlines, loss of interest, frustration, lethargy, apathy, exhaustion, anxiety and feeling a general sense of dissatisfaction with everything and everyone. If you sense that you are struggling with burnout, it often helps to identify those aspects in your job that excite you, intrigue you or give you a sense of energy. Perhaps it involves some new learning or interaction with interesting people. Arrange your time so that you can put what you enjoy into your schedule daily or as often as possible. It can also be helpful to pursue some outside activity that might interest you or about which you are enthusiastic. These things are all possible, but they take thought and planning. Sometimes, when suffering from burnout it becomes just another burden to have to think about it. Ask a close friend or your spouse to help you generate options to deal with it.

Your References: Your references set the stage for your acceptance in the organization—if they were incredibly glowing, they might generate unrealistic expectations that you are not aware of. If, however, there were reservations expressed, people will be especially primed to be on the lookout for those behaviors. They may see evidence even where none really exists, just because they are looking for it. Hopefully, you know what your references have said about you, because they have told you how they view your work at some time in the past. However, if you find that people are either expecting things from you that you never anticipated or acting as if they have some reservations about you, see if you can determine where that's coming from. The best way to do that is to talk with your supervisor. If that isn't helpful, try talking with one or two individuals whose judgment you are beginning to trust. Your reaction to any information you might get in these kinds of conversations is really important. You need to consider any information you receive as very helpful. Express your gratitude to the individuals who have trusted you enough to share what they know.

Reputation in the workplace: Most of the time references will work positively for you. We usually manage to build up a good reputation over our work life and that goes with us or even precedes us. Occasionally, word drifts into your new workplace from someone who is less than enthusiastic about you. Even more common, a remark has been conveyed to someone in the organization out of context and has been misconstrued. There are many types of situations that can occur. These are a few typical examples:

- Someone at your new workplace has a friend at your old place of employment. They call to find out about you. Something is said that has been interpreted as negative.

- A former client was upset with your former organization and blames you for the problem.

- Someone, who worked with you previously, now works in your new organization. They may feel that they need to tell everyone not only about your strengths, but also all the things they didn't think were so great.

- Your supervisor has related something you said in an interview to your work group. The comment has been repeated out of context.

Often in your interactions with your new work group, someone will obliquely refer to something related to you that just doesn't make any sense. If that happens, follow up with that individual to try to determine what he or she meant. Sometimes we are tempted to let these comments go by because we don't have a clue what they mean. We don't know what to say. In fact, however, the sooner you can find out what it all means, the faster you have an opportunity to provide a context that will be to your advantage.

Skeletons in THEIR Closet

Unfortunately, sometimes once you are a part of an organization, you begin to come across the skeletons in their closet. There is little that you can do about these skeletons except to figure out how to work with them or work around them. Some of the more frequent skeletons in the organization's closet are the following:

- Interpersonal or interdepartmental strife

- Individual or institutional bias

- Business problems

- Dishonest business practices

Interpersonal or interdepartmental strife: There can be a problem within a work group involving long-standing disagreements between two individuals. It may occur between departments, especially where two department heads are having an ongoing vendetta. Sometimes it involves a whole organization. The leadership may foster such competition among groups that working together to achieve results becomes difficult.

Usually this becomes obvious fairly quickly. People begin to refer to these situations fairly early on. Sometimes, however, they are never openly acknowledged and people go on acting as if they don't exist. You are asked to accomplish goals without any acknowledgment about the obstacles you will meet. Once you've recognized what is going on, your best options are to build as strong a personal relationship as you can with each of the factions. It also can help to identify those people in your group who seem to be able to operate well in this situation and observe how they handle it. Above all, do not take sides or get involved in any other way than trying to do the best job possible for everyone involved.

Individual or Institutional Bias: Sometimes you will find yourself in a group where individuals or the entire work group has a bias. This may not be a bias for which there is a legal remedy, but a bias that can get in your way. There may be a bias against outsiders, or people who are younger or people who didn't reach a certain level of education or people with a different point of view. The list could go on and on. Do not become involved with any biased behavior. If the bias happens to be against you, do what you can to build individual working relationships one by one. Also try to understand what the real objection is behind the bias. Usually a bias is a catchall for certain behaviors that the individual or the group finds irritating.

Business Problems

Sometimes you enter an organization and find that business problems exist that were not disclosed to you in the pre-hire process. This situation has the potential to make your job more difficult or give you a greater opportunity for challenge and success. Your best option is to try to fully understand the situation as quickly as possible so you can focus your work towards real solutions. This involves getting many different perspectives on the problem and sifting through them to come to your own conclusions. If, however, you continue to have a feeling that the organization is being less than forthright with you over a period of time, and that you are working in the dark, it's a serious issue and certainly reason to make plans to look for other opportunities elsewhere.

Dishonest Business Practices

Do not jump to conclusions. Sometimes when you are new, you are asked to do something that doesn't seem right to you because you do not fully understand the situation. However, this does not mean that you have to go ahead and do it without understanding enough to feel comfortable. Be sure to ask questions and talk to others whose judgment seems sound. In certain circumstances, it may even be necessary to seek outside legal counsel at your own expense. If you do not get answers that satisfy you, do not do anything that you think could compromise your career or your personal integrity. Under no circumstances is it ever all right to be asked to be a participant in a dishonest business practice.

KEY QUESTIONS

WEEK THREE

1. Do you have any personal problems, distractions or responsibilities that are making it more difficult for you to do your job well? How can you best manage them?*

2. Are you responding to your job in a way that makes you think you are suffering from burnout?*

3. Do you have friends or family who can help you?

4. Do co-workers seem to expect skills that you don't have such as computer skills, presentation skills, a certain professional image?

5. Do co-workers seem to expect you to do work or spend time in a way different from your expectations?*

6. Are you getting consistently unusual, unpredictable or "off the wall" responses from individuals you work with?*

7. Are you getting negative feedback or negative responses from supervisors or co-workers?*

8. Is the group in a crisis mode or does the environment seem stable?

9. Do you see a lot of interpersonal conflicts, grandstanding or an obvious need to control events on the part of some individuals?

10. Have you been approached by anyone asking you to take sides?

11. Do you find yourself frequently being blocked by several warring factions, when you try to accomplish your work?

12. Do you find that you're frequently not being included in the information loop?

13. Has something previously promised you, like a job assignment or a pay increase, been withdrawn without explanation or reason?

14. Have you been asked to do anything that seems contrary to ethical business practice? If so, is there someone you can trust to talk to about it, who is also knowledgeable about such things?

SUGGESTIONS FOR ACTION

WEEK THREE

- If personal problems seem overwhelming, make it a top priority to get help and keep your supervisor informed.

- Look for those people with a balanced input and values that you can trust to help you understand what's going on.

- Work on developing relationships of trust with several people.

- Try to experience people with whom you have a very negative or positive feeling in multiple contexts, i.e. lunch, meetings, one-on- one, coffee. Work to understand their perspective.

- Look behind comments and advice for veiled meaning. Who is it coming from? Get others' perspectives.

- If someone is consistently treating you poorly, set up a time to talk with him/her and ask how you can make the working relationship better.

- Once you have tried to change a situation and communication still breaks down, ask for a third party intervention, for example, a human resource person.

- Do not ignore problems or negative signals. Unresolved issues seldom get better on their own.

- Do not let other people define how you evaluate people, although be open to listening to whatever information comes your way.

- If you are seriously concerned about potential violation of your professional or personal ethics seek outside guidance or counsel.

"In the main, I'm the driving force for taking something that does not exist to a product." —Carol G

"If you are at the right place at the right time and you can share information with people when they need it, all of a sudden you become this really valued employee." —Mara

WEEK FOUR

Your Value Added

Now is the time to deliver on the reasons you were chosen to fill the position. It's important to direct your special skills and abilities to whatever you have identified as most important to the company and yourself. Look back on the job description that you have been creating. What has emerged for you as being most important? Where do you see putting your effort that will bring you the greatest sense of achievement and sense of satisfaction?

It is also important to direct your abilities to what your boss, your internal clients, your external clients and your co-workers have identified as most important. We'll refer to all these groups as stakeholders. If you have been including their inputs into your creation of a job description, you should have some ideas about their priorities by now.

Sometimes it's fairly straightforward to move ahead because all those involved share similar goals. Sometimes it's much more difficult because the different stakeholders have very different priorities. In this kind of situation, it is important to find some common ground between the stakeholders and some mutually important goals that they can agree on. They need to be mutual goals that are top priority to each group. One way to approach this conundrum is to work toward getting agreement from all parties on three of your major responsibilities. Gaining agreement can be a challenging process, but it is extremely important. Only when you have clarity about your direction and role can you be effective.

> *"I try to understand things from other people's point of view. As we share ideas, there becomes a collaboration." —Greg R*

As you go through discussions with different stakeholders, it's also helpful to identify any processes or systems that could get in the way of accomplishing what you set out to do. Ask people what obstacles might stand in your way. If obstacles seem obvious to you, bring them up and ask for help in removing them. People are often eager to help, if you are working toward common goals.

Once you feel fairly confident of where your energies and skills need to be directed, use all your capabilities as quickly as possible to demonstrate that you are going to bring value. Use the abilities that you most enjoy, because that will make the job more satisfying. Start building key collaborations to accomplish what needs to be done.

> *"I couldn't disengage because that would be death to my job. So I decided I would do the best job I could and kept trying to engage people to work toward cooperation." —Linda*

We're all unique and bring special strengths to whatever we do. We're also not perfect. As you direct your energies and strengths towards what's important, it's equally as important to acknowledge any weaknesses you might have. It was suggested in "Knowing Yourself" that you give some thought to your downsides and how to manage them. Now that you know more about the job and the requirements, you know more about any projects, processes or personal qualities needed that do not play to your strengths. They may be things you don't like to do, things you don't do well or skills that need some sharpening. There may be situations where your personal style is not a good fit. Devise a plan to deal with these situations. Solutions usually involve finding help, exchanging your skills with someone else, or improving your skills through practice, classes or special tutoring.

While you are thinking about the value you add to the organization, be sure to consider your role as a team member. Make sure there is clarity about what role you are to assume. What can you bring to the team to help them function well? You may have skills in helping people integrate their ideas or moving group processes along. Each of us usually plays a unique role in the process of the group. Make sure that your role is a useful one. Be sensitive to how the team responds to you. You will begin to see what the group perceives as helpful versus what the group perceives as putting obstacles in the way. Be careful to ensure that you never accomplish anything at someone else's expense.

Of course you have been working hard to add value to the organization from the moment you started on the job. One of the things that we all can do early on is to be open and freely share information with others, which can help them achieve their goals. Certainly applying any of your skills to help any of the stakeholders sends the message that you are there to bring value in whatever way you can. It often takes a number of weeks or even months, however, to really understand what your greatest contribution can be. It is an evolving process and will go on throughout the time you are in the organization. Be mindful of any changes you make in terms of the impact and timing. Keep in mind that you have a powerful ally in this effort. Most employers want to believe that they made the right choice in bringing you into the organization. Your performance reflects on their judgment. This gives you an immediate advantage.

KEY QUESTIONS

WEEK FOUR

1. How can you best use your strengths?*

2. How can you minimize your downsides?*

3. What role do you need to take to make the job work?*

4. What are your **three** major responsibilities:*

   - As seen by your supervisor/boss?

   - As seen by your co-workers?

   - As seen by your internal clients?

   - As seen by your external clients?

5. How do you bring the above together so there is no disconnect?

6. Having considered the information in #4 and #5, where do you most want to put your efforts? What areas fit best with your abilities? Are there areas you have to shore up due to a lack of skill, ability or experience?*

7. What stands in the way of getting this job done? Is it possible for anyone to do this job the way it is expected to be done?*

8. If a team is involved, what important role do you need to play as a team member?

9. Where have you been able to make an immediate positive impact?*

SUGGESTIONS FOR ACTION

WEEK FOUR

- Apply what you've done before to make it happen, but be sure that it is appropriately adapted to the new situation.

- Find ways to make yourself indispensable.

- Define clearly what is realistic and not realistic. Renegotiate where you need to.

- Acknowledge what you don't do well and devise a plan to deal with it.

  - Find coaching or classes.

  - Find people who are willing to help you.

- Develop a barter system (e.g., help someone with a presentation that you can do in exchange for a budget forecast).

- If you are a supervisor, hire staff that has complementary talents.

- Do not ignore problem areas. Work with someone else to find solutions. The longer you pretend they are not there, the worse it is when you finally have to resolve them.

- Be sure your strengths are applied toward outcomes that are important and related.

"The biggest positive is that at a pebble at a time, we are making progress...many, many small wins." —Linda

"The assignment is well within my capabilities and track record...I'm very confident I can do it." —Greg W

"If someone is not returning your call the first time, call again. Don't take no for an answer first blush. Pursue it beyond that.." —Steve

"I'm trying to give myself a little slack...a little permission that I just might not meet my quota by the end of the year." —Tricia

WEEK FIVE

Productivity—Your Sense of Accomplishment

In previous chapters, we have seen activities that build on your strengths and use them in achieving organizational priorities. You've looked at ways to have impact. You've looked at achieving results that generate a sense of accomplishment.

New employees do have a slight advantage. You get a chance to learn the lay of the land and you're not expected to produce at peak levels right away or make too many fast and impactful changes. Nevertheless, the sooner you can make a significant contribution, the sooner you will establish your credibility with the group.

It's important that you establish a solid sense of accomplishment and begin to feel productive. Key to achieving significant accomplishment is setting the right goals. Hopefully by now, you have included many groups in your discussions, in your efforts to determine your value added. You probably now have all the information you need to set goals. Naturally, the most effective and most motivating goals are relevant, time-based, measurable and specific. Well-crafted goal statements provide a source of feedback, accountability and evaluation. In writing and creating them, you might want to work independently at first and then talk out your drafts with your boss or a trusted co-worker.

Research on goal setting emphasizes relevancy. You want to work on projects that not only interest *you* but also have organizational impact and link to agreed upon organizational initiatives. They should also highlight your skill set and provide you opportunities to receive feedback. Build in deadlines that are attainable yet of moderate risk. Allow adequate time to prove yourself and enough stretch in your workload to create a satisfying challenge. Include criteria for determining whether or not you have achieved your goals. Getting commitment to your goals from your supervisor builds in support for the results.

Be open to both positive and corrective feedback. Both are important to your success.

It's again a time to be tuned into the reactions of the group and messages they may be sending you. Some co-workers might be threatened by your work. They may be withholding information or input that could help. Others may not be helpful just because they are not clear on what you are doing, or what you need from them. Keep the communication channels open and catch things quickly by asking for feedback. Make the effort to constantly clarify and match or exceed the organization's standards for quality. Everyone should be in agreement on what quality looks like, and your standards should be in sync with what your supervisor and key customers have agreed upon.

Finding the time to build all the working relationships you need to when you first come into an organization and still be able to be productive is a challenge. However you need those relationships to help enhance your productivity. There needs to be balance. You need to walk the fine line between developing relationships and developing productivity.

Productivity is a two-way street. Not only are you achieving something for the organization, you're achieving something for yourself.

KEY QUESTIONS

WEEK FIVE

1. What have you been able to accomplish to date?

2. How do you feel about what you've been able to do?*

3. How have you built on your strengths and experience to accomplish what you've achieved?

4. Have you discussed your level of achievement with your supervisor?*

5. Have you received feedback, either verbal or nonverbal from others?*

6. How much support did you get from others toward your progress so far?

7. Do your standards for quality work seem to match the group supervisor's and customer's standards? Do you notice differences between their standards and yours?

8. Contrast your ability to contribute and achieve with what's required by the workplace.

9. Are you doing work that you feel is important and has impact?

10. Is there a reasonable balance between your relationships and your productivity?

SUGGESTIONS FOR ACTION

WEEK FIVE

- Stay tuned to the balance between relationship and productivity.

- Monitor your time and use it wisely.

- Talk to your supervisor now about his/her perspective on your productivity.

- Listen to how people describe you as they introduce you to others or at meetings.*

- Watch and listen for signals of impatience or need for extended deadlines. Be sure that the majority of these are not due to your shortcomings.

- Keep a written record or work completed on time and on target. A list of goal accomplishments should be visible in your work area.

- Be mindful of rework that others are asking you to do. If you are getting a lot of rework, look for the real problem.

- Listen to how you answer when people ask you if you like your job.*

- Pass on any praise for your accomplishments to people who helped you. Make it a group accomplishment/achievement. Share the praise.

- Don't take yourself too seriously.

"My evaluation of the job basically has to do with feeling or instinct. If I feel thwarted, if I feel unhappy, if I'm not developing, then I take some action to try to make things go in the direction I want. The last thing I want is to do the job and be resentful about it." —Greg R

"Based on the criteria set beforehand everything's been met so far. I don't know the technology as well as I'd like." —Kay

"The workload was more severe than anticipated, and the computer component more substantial. There's an information overload, as well." —Ray

WEEK SIX

Time To Take Stock

You've been around awhile and have a sense of how things are going. There are probably lots of feelings that are surfacing and certain perceptions about your job that are forming. A reading of your *Transition Journal* and any other notes you've been taking will give you a rough picture or a snapshot. No doubt your range of emotions have been all over the map. Perhaps that initial and typical nervousness or concern has subsided. Maybe it's intensified. You may be feeling more comfortable and involved, or disappointed and undervalued. Quite often our feelings are manifested in our pace, energy or stress levels.

Indeed, now may also be an appropriate time to assess your situation more systematically or formally. Much research has been done about job satisfaction and what makes us happy in our work. We have broken these into four major categories:

- The company—its values and its culture.

- The job itself—what you've been doing, what you've been able to accomplish.

- The work group—the relationships fostered, the support and encouragement received.

- The supervisor—the rapport, the trust, the feedback that's created.

Complete the index on the next page as another step in taking stock of your situation. It's a great opportunity to check out how you're feeling at this point in time.

SATISFACTION INDEX

For each of the following questions, please circle the response that in your opinion best answers the question.

1 = Never *2* = Seldom *3* = Sometimes *4* = Often *5* = Always

1. I trust most of the people I work with.

    1   **2**   **3**   **4**   **5**

2. I have the opportunity to meet with my co-workers.

    1   **2**   **3**   **4**   **5**

3. My associates involve me in decisions that are important to my job.

    1   **2**   **3**   **4**   **5**

4. I receive positive feedback from my work group for assignments well done.

    1   **2**   **3**   **4**   **5**

5. My co-workers offer helpful suggestions on how to improve my work.

    1   **2**   **3**   **4**   **5**

6. I enjoy being with my co-workers.

    1   **2**   **3**   **4**   **5**

7. My supervisor provides needed help.

    1   **2**   **3**   **4**   **5**

8   I can see how my supervisor eliminates barriers for me to get work accomplished.

    1   **2**   **3**   **4**   **5**

9. I can trust my supervisor.

1   **2**   **3**   **4**   **5**

10. My supervisor recognizes my accomplishments.

1   **2**   **3**   **4**   **5**

11. I receive appropriate constructive criticism from my supervisor.

1   **2**   **3**   **4**   **5**

12. My supervisor involves me in important decisions relating to my job.

1   **2**   **3**   **4**   **5**

13. My supervisor responds to my suggestions.

1   **2**   **3**   **4**   **5**

14. My supervisor contributes to making my work fun.

1   **2**   **3**   **4**   **5**

15. My work is making a contribution to the success of the organization.

1   **2**   **3**   **4**   **5**

16. I like coming to work each day.

1   **2**   **3**   **4**   **5**

17. My assignments tap my strongest skills.

1   **2**   **3**   **4**   **5**

18. I am able to handle the administrative/paperwork part of my job.

1   **2**   **3**   **4**   **5**

19. I am making a difference with my work.

1　　　　**2**　　　　**3**　　　　**4**　　　　**5**

20. The organization provides a quality product or service.

1　　　　**2**　　　　**3**　　　　**4**　　　　**5**

21. I feel that upper management listens to my opinions.

1　　　　**2**　　　　**3**　　　　**4**　　　　**5**

22. Our product or service is represented truthfully in the marketplace.

1　　　　**2**　　　　**3**　　　　**4**　　　　**5**

23. My organization allows me to reach my full potential.

1　　　　**2**　　　　**3**　　　　**4**　　　　**5**

24. The communication channels in my organization make it easy for me to get my job done.

1　　　　**2**　　　　**3**　　　　**4**　　　　**5**

25. The executives in our organization show positive ways of interacting with other people in the organization.

1　　　　**2**　　　　**3**　　　　**4**　　　　**5**

26. I see the organization fostering trust and collaboration.

1　　　　**2**　　　　**3**　　　　**4**　　　　**5**

27. I see my personal values consistent with the values of the organization

1　　　　**2**　　　　**3**　　　　**4**　　　　**5**

28. My organization contributes to the betterment of the community.

1　　　　**2**　　　　**3**　　　　**4**　　　　**5**

TOTALS:

A quick total of your score will indicate where you stand.

Add the numbers up: _____

If your figures total from **112 to 140**, your results are *moderate* to *high*.

If your figures total from **84 to 112**, your results are *moderate*.

If your figures total **0 to 84**, your results are *moderate* to *low*.

SUGGESTIONS FOR ACTION

MODERATE TO HIGH

Unless your instincts or feelings don't agree with the results of
this survey, continue doing what you're doing at work and move
directly to Part Three of this book.

SUGGESTIONS FOR ACTION

MODERATE

Choose three ways that you feel good about the job or successful
in the job. Then focus on building and making them even more
satisfying.

SUGGESTIONS FOR ACTION

MODERATE TO LOW

1. Choose three areas where you feel improvement must take place for you to be able to stay in the job.

2. Address one area each month over the next three months.

3. Devise a plan of action and follow through.

4. In creating your action plan, remember to do the following:

   - Focus on the problem. Clarify and re-clarify until you are satisfied that you understand what is actually bothering you.

   - Be clear about where change is actually possible. Be honest with yourself if you simply do not have the ability or desire to make change happen.

   - Validate your information and planning process with a trusted friend, spouse, partner or career counselor.

   - Talk to your supervisor. Discuss issues and ways to resolve them, such as:

     ♦ Restructuring the job in the near term.

     ♦ Restructuring the job over a longer period or moving to another job over an agreed upon period of time.

     ♦ Volunteering to work on a team or special task force to use and demonstrate skills.

     ♦ Taking on a special project that will allow you to use and demonstrate skills.

To help the above discussion go well, take responsibility for any problems and work toward a positive outcome.

5. Once your plan is developed, act upon it.

6. Remember throughout this process that you are indeed in control and can take action to follow through. Ignoring the issues will not make them go away, unless they exist with individuals you feel are leaving the work group soon.

PART THREE:

FROM SIX WEEKS TO THREE MONTHS

"It's definitely important to build strong relationships throughout the company; these people can be your greatest resource." —Steve

"I've been asking a lot of questions, networking, and leveraging off peers." —Kay

"There are things I personally choose to do and they are never in the job description, but they are part of me and therefore part of what I bring to a company. Part of that is giving back to the community."—Carol G

Expanding Your Influence

Once you begin to master your work and see productive results, it's important to look beyond your immediate work group or sphere of contact. Success often requires exposure to various parts of the organization. Your participation in different activities and contribution to special assignments can increase the likelihood of career mobility and bring additional reward and satisfaction to your work life. Research on long-term organizational commitment and employee loyalty always includes participation and/or involvement as a key ingredient. It can be reflected in anything from making a decision to promoting a corporate value. When you are on solid footing and satisfied with your results to date, the time might be right for additional exposure.

You may begin by examining how your work affects people in other divisions or off-site locations. Exactly *when* to do this, however, is a tough call. If you begin too early, the additional work can shift your focus and derail you from the important direct job results. If you wait too long, you can miss valuable opportunities and information that you might need both in the long and short term. It's a fine line but one well worth walking.

Certainly you can benefit in other ways besides the satisfaction that comes from participation. There are new relationships and potential friendships to be made. There's potential to make a bond with a new group of people who will know you and your work. There are chances to have fun, strengthen a skill or pursue a hobby. There's new information to learn that can increase your understanding of the business and add to your value as a decision maker. You will be offered a wider perspective and thus become a more effective problem solver. You're likely to learn something about your job that could *only* come from an exposure to other parts of the company. This can give you a better idea of how your group contributes to the whole organization. It can help you be more productive. The organizatin benefits as well. It brings people together for cross-functional work and generates greater efficiencies and economies of scale. It fosters camaraderie and opens people up to new work and new opportunities. It provides vehicles for employees to grow.

Eventually, your involvement may extend beyond the organization and into the community. There your work brings another source of business intelligence and market data to the table. When you volunteer for a non-profit, sit on a board of directors or head an activity with your children. Although you collect data informally, you can still pick up valuable competitive information. At the same time, you are a walking advertisement for your organization and bring recognition and positive goodwill by your contributions and dedication.

All these additional efforts can bring rewards, if you truly enjoy them and are sincerely interested. Balance is important. These activities need to bring as much to your life and satisfaction as they bring to the organization.

Building expanded alliances and the networking that comes with it is an important part of your career management process. It can be done once you are comfortable with your productivity and the relationships fostered in your immediate work group. Take your cue for managing these efforts from the culture and values of the organization.

KEY QUESTIONS

EXPANDING YOUR INFLUENCE

1. How does your work impact people in other divisions or areas?

2. What have you done to build relationships beyond your immediate scope?

3. Is it usual or unusual for people in your organization to build relationships beyond their immediate scope?

4. What opportunities do you see to expand your network of working relationships in the organization and in the community?

5. How can you combine reaching out with your existing job assignment?*

6. Is there a way to meet some of your satisfaction needs on the job through other activities in the organization?*

7. Is your organization associated with a cause or community involvement project that you can identify with?

8. How does your supervisor model organization participation?

SUGGESTIONS FOR ACTION

EXPANDING YOUR INFLUENCE

- Be sure your commitment to extending yourself has a real basis or reason. It can be unfortunate if people feel you are only reaching out because you're trying to impact your job status or political standing.

- Be sure that these commitments and new activities enhance your work and do not stand in the way of accomplishing other necessary parts of your work load or solidifying key work group relationships.

- Some ways to become involved are:

  - Joining a cross-functional team to solve a particular problem

  - Volunteering for a cross company event or special group

  - Donating time to a company sponsored commitment

  - Attending informal meetings with senior officers

  - Getting involved with a company sponsored United Way drive

  - Signing up for special projects in your own group or division

  - Keep your supervisor informed about any of your involvements. Avoid any surprises.

"My perspective changed pretty quickly especially about the 'perks' (stocks, options, etc.). I am also working much more with the #1 person than with my former contact who brought me into the organization. I hadn't counted on that. One is 'hands-on'; the other is 'hands-off.'" —Tricia

*"It's not effective to come in and do it your way right away. Take time to learn and understand the processes **before** doing anything or making any changes."* —Kay

Change Happens

All of us respond differently to change and we resist it in varying degrees. Some, though, thrive on things being a little different all the time. Others take a while to adjust to anything that's new or different from the familiar or from what they had expected and bargained for. Change for many is a loss of control. In the big scheme of things or macro view, a new job or position is a major shift, but even within that context, many things can happen to reshape or alter the situation once we have begun. How we respond and handle our resistance can be a powerful indicator of our success.

Find Out What The Change Is.

There are many things you can do to work out or deal with the changes that can come up at this point. The first is to find out *what* exactly is different. It may be simple or complex. In either case, anything you can do to gather all the information will be helpful. The assignment you have worked on so diligently may no longer be necessary, or your work in progress could be terminated. Maybe there's been an economic downturn or lots of turnover. It could even be a shift in the corporate direction or a change in leadership. Knowing as much as you can is important. Information can be power in this situation. Knowledge often helps bring control.

Why Has The Change Happened?

Ask questions to find out and understand **why** the changes occurred. Understanding can help with our nervousness or uncertainty. Obviously, the more you know the impact of the change, the better you will be able to adjust your behavior.

How does the change Affect Us.

How are the changes affecting you or your group? How are others reacting or responding? How are you working out your disappointments, etc.? Be sure that there are no misunderstandings about what's going on.

Solve Problem Positively

Finally, making every effort to solve problems related to the change will engage you and encourage you to move forward. Support and commitment are key ingredients to solving problems positively. If you understand what the changes are and why they are taking place, you can resolve any possible misunderstandings. Then you can indeed move forward.

When initiating change, you must be especially tuned into the timing of your actions and the sensitivity of your implementation. Very often one is hired to make changes or to move things in a different direction. Gathering data and putting our "ducks in a row" must be the first order of business before any action is taken:

- Be aware of the challenge and what you are up against. You must be clear that what you want to do differently is meeting this challenge in a productive way.

- You must control and manage the process. Solicit questions, answer them directly and honestly and provide all the information necessary to be sure there is clarity.

- Spell out the positives and the negatives of the change in a realistic and logical way.

- Ask for support and buy-in, and be there to explain and talk out the issues.

Be sure to keep in mind that it is essential to build commitment within the organization. Be careful not to make any drastic changes until research has been done, the appropriate connections have been made and you have built the necessary commitment.

KEY QUESTIONS

CHANGE

1. Is the amount of change happening comfortable or uncomfortable?*

2. In what areas do you see the change taking place?

3. How does the change impact your workload?

4. Is the workload still realistic?

5. How do the changes impact your level of satisfaction with your work and work environment?*

6. What changes need to be made for you to be more effective or work more efficiently?

7. How can the change help you grow personally and professionally?*

8. Is there any disadvantage to adapting to the change?

SUGGESTIONS FOR ACTION

CHANGE

When change happens to you:

- Try to detach yourself. Try not to become so attached to any direction, approach or procedure that you can't give it up.

- Accept the reality that things **will** be different.

- Get the answers you need to understand the change and cope with it. Ask a lot of why's (but not the same ones, over and over) and be comfortable with the replies. When it is clear the change will happen, accept it and move on.

- Save all the work you've done, even if it is no longer needed. You might need it again or be required to work on an assignment so similar that this material can save you a lot of work later on.

- Try to bring some kind of closure to the experience so that you don't keep rehashing it.

- Allow time and give yourself permission to 'grieve' for what's lost or has been taken away.

- Use your Journal/Diary as a way to describe what is going on for you and to "vent".

When you make the change:

- Be clear about why you want the change.

- Have a strong rationale and substantive data to back up your thoughts and ideas.

- Be specific about who will be impacted and how.

- Try to get partners for the change one on one before you announce it to the group.

- Seek input on the change one on one from those who will be most impacted by the outcome.

Find the Bathrooms First!

- Be mindful that there are usually negatives in every change as well as positives and surface both honestly. Be prepared to deal with the negatives.

- Be objective and don't let your personal bias, need or ambition drive you to ignore or unduly pressure others.

- Be prepared for the most-often-asked questions and be ready to respond non-defensively.

- Give thought to and choose the most effective forms of communication for letting people know about the change. Vary your approach to ensure that all affected can understand the implications.

- Never act unilaterally unless no one else is impacted by the change.

- After the change is initiated, monitor the progress of the change and follow up to handle problems or issues.

"The Key Question is, will the small wins be enough for me to want to continue in this job long term"? —Linda

"My weaknesses have yet to be an issue. There's a 70% success rate, since there are new areas for me to learn." —Kay

Are We Having Fun Yet?

This book has covered the first three months on the job because it is such a pivotal time for laying a strong foundation for your success, for making this a meaningful step in your career and for learning about yourself. At about 90 days or three months, a gut level sense begins to develop. You begin to get a feeling that either the job's going to work out, or it's not right. It's important not to ignore these feelings. If you are happy in your new position, it's helpful to try to understand why. This is information that can help you understand more about what works for you, or what you can make more workable. If you are feeling uncomfortable or disappointed with your job, these feelings also give you insight into the real source of the discontent. In addition, if you are unhappy, there is a strong possibility that the organization may not be satisfied with you. The two don't always go together, but they often do. By facing the reality of your situation, you have more of an opportunity to take the appropriate action. There is greater potential to have more control over your own destiny. By taking action at this time, you give yourself the best chance to stay in charge of fully directing and managing your own career.

The key to making any decision about your career is the degree to which you feel a sense of satisfaction with the position you have and the organization you have joined. The blueprint for satisfaction is different for each person. We talked in **Week Six: Time to Take Stock** about certain basic factors that lead to job satisfaction: the values and culture of the organization, the content of the job, the relationship with your workgroup and the relationship with your boss. A sense of satisfaction also involves:

- Your personality and the work environment.

- Respect for yourself and the organization.

Your Personality And The Work Environment

Each of us has requirements that we most need from our work environment. These are based on our personal preferences. For some it's a quiet and orderly place to think and work. For others it's a busy, fast-paced environment with a lot of interaction. Some of us need to get results above all else. Others need to focus on the methods used to get the results. Some people love group decision-making. Others need to make decisions in a more contemplative, solidary manner. Some people need to be giving and getting constant feedback. Others neither want to give or get much feedback. The amount of control that one needs over the scope and direction of his or her work is different for each individual. Some people need to have complete control over how the work is done and the result. Others like the challenge of dealing with the unexpected on a daily basis.

Each person needs to identify the factors in the environment that are necessary for job satisfaction. If you haven't given thought to what you need, it's important to do that now. When your personal style is a good fit, the work you are doing and the people you are doing it with will give you energy. If, on the other hand, you leave work everyday feeling really tired and dispirited, the chances are that your personal style does not match the environment. Give thought to where the disconnects may be. Decide if it's possible to change yourself or the situation enough to make it work for you.

Respect For Yourself and The Organization

Respect is a vital element for everyone in any work environment. No matter what other factors are right about the job, it is very difficult to maintain your self-esteem or care about the job that you do unless you work in an environment of mutual respect. An environment of respect includes:

- Respect for yourself.
    1. Respect for the work you are doing.
    2. Respect for the people you work with.
    3. Respect for the leadership of the organization.

Each person wants to be treated with respect. We all want to have our ideas and our contributions acknowledged. We want to be able to present the work that we do as our own. We want to be recognized for the quality of our work. Most of us want the people we work with to, at a minimum, value the same things that we value about ourselves.

In addition, we want to respect the people with whom we work. We want to be able to feel that they have something to contribute. We would like to be able to get ideas and suggestions from them. We would like to learn from them. We want to work with people whose values, actions, and thinking we can respect.

Lastly, it is important to respect the leadership of the organization and the individual in charge of our own work group. We want the leadership in our organization to have thinking that is realistic and balanced. We want leaders whose word and commitment we can trust. We want leaders who are positive and optimistic, but don't wear rose-colored glasses. We want leaders who accept responsibility for their own mistakes and back us up when we take agreed upon risks. Most of all, we want leaders who display consistency. People we can count on.

There is no perfect environment and no perfect organization. However most of us need to have some combination of the factors that make up respect. Which factors these are is an individual choice that can only be evaluated by the person involved. Everyone deserves to work in an environment where he or she is respected. No one can continue to function well for very long in an environment that erodes his or her self-esteem!

In **Week Six: Time To Take Stock**, you did an interim assessment of how the job was meeting your needs. Now is the time to take a more serious look at whether this job is the right one for you. Do you look forward to going to work? Do you get a sense of energy from your work?

- Do you get more of a feeling of energy from work when you have a lot of interaction with other people during the day, or when you have more time alone and work on your own?

- Do you get enough opportunity to think through your work quietly?

- Do you need to take action and get closure? If so, is there an adequate amount of action and closure in this job?

- Do you prefer to focus on the process of achieving the job? If so, do you have enough of an opportunity to help structure how the results are achieved?

- Do you need to be in constant control of your work, or do you prefer to let whatever happens take its course?

- Do you tend to get hooked on trying to prove to people that you're O.K., especially when they have negative opinions of you?

- How do you react to feedback? Do you consider it as data? Are you more prone to remember and respond to positive feedback?

- How do your personal values impact your decisions?

- Do you tend to make decisions based more on gut level feelings or data that you collect?

- What does your decision history tell you about how you make decisions? What has worked well for you in the past?

Using the information you got about yourself above, move on to the **Key Questions** and **Suggestions for Action.**

KEY QUESTIONS

HAVING FUN YET?

1. How do you feel about the people you work with and your working relationships?

2. Is the work environment compatible with your personal requirements?*

3. Is the feedback you're getting encouraging or discouraging?*

4. Are the opportunities you hoped for actually available?*

5. Is your current salary satisfactory to meet your needs at this time?

6. Do you feel more confident or less confident since you came to this job?*

7. Are you getting an adequate sense of satisfaction out of your job?

8. If you aren't, are the blocks to your satisfaction realistically movable or immovable?

SUGGESTIONS FOR ACTION

HAVING FUN YET?

- Makes a list: **Reasons To Commit To This Job.**

- Makes a list: **Reasons To Think About Other Job Options.**

- Resolve any interpersonal problems to your satisfaction. Either change your perception of the problem or work with the individuals involved to find a resolution.

Look over the Satisfaction Index you completed in **Time To Take Stock.** To help determine your current level of satisfaction, retake the Satisfaction Index at the end of this chapter. Compare with the last Index you took to assess for any changes.

It makes sense to stay with the position if you have most of the following:

- ♦ Your score on the Satisfaction Index is moderate to high.

- ♦ You find that your values match those of the organization.

- ♦ You enjoy the work that you are doing.

- ♦ People you work with appreciate your efforts.

- ♦ You and your supervisor are beginning to form a partnership.

- ♦ You get support from your supervisor.

- Most of the time you look forward to going to work.

- You respect the people you work with and the organization you work for.

It's time to consider leaving the job if you are getting the following warning signs:

- Your score on the Satisfaction Index is moderate to low.

- The blocks to your satisfaction seem insurmountable.

- You dread going to work and/or you find yourself getting depressed.

- You are losing confidence in yourself.

- The people you work with, including your supervisor, have adopted a negative attitude toward you that you think you cannot change.

Your Options for Action:*

- Commit fully to the job.

- Give it a little more time, with a plan to resolve any existing problems.

- Begin looking within the organization for other opportunities. **

- Begin looking outside the company. **

** Both of these can be done at the same time.

"I'm much more flexible than I thought, and the challenges were not as scary as they seemed." —Kay

"There's an introspection here that wasn't there before. I know what I'm doing, and I'm moving forward. I'm focused now and feel a real sense of purpose. It's important I make a real success out of this phase of my life. I realize that." —John

"I can't change as much as I'd like to. I'm learning to appreciate my abilities more, but my personal style things can't change" —Greg W

What You've Learned About Yourself

Indeed, each of our life experiences teaches us different things. Because of our own special qualities, we all take away something different from the same basic experiences. When a family moves to a new city, each member generates different reactions and feelings, though everyone must learn how to make new friends or find important local resources. We marry or move in with a "significant other" and learn how to compromise and work out the day-to-day issues of living with another person. We change jobs and learn a set of new tasks and procedures or adapt to a different set of cultural norms.

In addition, we take away personal learnings regarding our abilities to accomplish what we want or our skills to make new friends or influence decisions. A new position, for many, is an opportunity to learn, practice or shift behaviors. Sometimes it is easier to change when we enter a situation fresh and can be a bit more receptive and able to behave differently. We are never too old or too set in our ways that we can't learn. We must constantly look to the future in managing our careers and the learning skills that will continue to move us forward. What we learn from this experience can be applied to any future professional opportunity. What have you learned from the experience? What have you learned about yourself?

KEY QUESTIONS

WHAT YOU'VE LEARNED

1. What have proven to be your greatest strengths in making this job transition?*

2. What do you need to change about yourself to be more effective in the job?*

3. What external factors have you discovered are most important to you at this point in your life?

4. What have you learned about future career choices?*

    ♦ Type of supervisor you like to work with or absolutely cannot work with.

    ♦ Opportunities to be an individual performer vs. a group leader.

    ♦ Preference for a small organization vs. a large one.

5. What have you found is most helpful to you in assessing and making solid career choices?*

6. What kind of work group culture is so important to you that you won't compromise on it?*

7. What has been really successful for you in this job transition?*

8. What would you never do again?*

9. Where could you have saved yourself worry about things that never happened?*

SUGGESTIONS FOR ACTION

WHAT YOU'VE LEARNED

- Review your *Transition Journal* thoroughly, searching for themes that run throughout. Underline, asterisk, or watch for repetition of key words or similar thoughts.

- List five things you have to have in a job in order of priority.*

- List three things you are most proud of accomplishing.*

- Realize that you have not only made the best effort to make this career opportunity successful, but you have also prepared yourself for your next career opportunity.

The things that can be learned are as individual as each person. There are no limits.

"This is the first time I've had the opportunity to do the whole job. I'm now in a place where I have the opportunity to create. I'm learning a lot." —Linda

"I've learned more about my vulnerability and fear of failure; more about taking risks for a job." —Tricia

"I'm more true to myself—less afraid of my gut perceptions; satisfied with the direction." —Jules

"I've learned to look for positives. I find that when I look for the negatives about the company and the people in it, it just makes me miserable. Now I try to understand things from other people's point of view." —Greg R

"I learned how hard I took the layoff after 14 years. There was a devastating loss of identity." —Genetha

"I learned I'm more flexible and resilient than I thought. I rose to the challenge. I can succeed at something new." —Ray

"I learned that moving to a new area and leaving my old life was much more difficult than I had expected. It was my biggest surprise about taking the job." —Steve

"I've learned that before you accept a job you need to know about the culture of the company and whether it's panic driven." —Maureen

"I want to move to a small company where the level of responsibility and challenge will be greater." —Steve

"I now see that I was too mellow for too long; it made it almost impossible to gain control of an area that I thought was going to be mine."
—Carol G

"I've really grown, and I've learned to filter things out that bother me and come to compromise with people." —Mara

"I've learned that whether I succeed or not, my job is my responsibility."
—Greg R

SATISFACTION INDEX

For each of the following questions, please circle the response that in your opinion best answers the question.

1 = Never **2** = Seldom **3** = Sometimes **4** = Often **5** = Always

1. I trust most of the people I work with.

   1   **2**   **3**   **4**   **5**

2. I have the opportunity to meet with my co-workers.

   1   **2**   **3**   **4**   **5**

3. My associates involve me in decisions that are important to my job.

   1   **2**   **3**   **4**   **5**

4. I receive positive feedback from my work group for assignments well done.

   1   **2**   **3**   **4**   **5**

5. My co-workers offer helpful suggestions on how to improve my work.

   1   **2**   **3**   **4**   **5**

6. I enjoy being with my co-workers.

   1   **2**   **3**   **4**   **5**

7. My supervisor provides needed help.

   1   **2**   **3**   **4**   **5**

8. I can see how my supervisor eliminates barriers for me to get work accomplished.

   1   **2**   **3**   **4**   **5**

9. I can trust my supervisor.

1   **2**   **3**   **4**   **5**

10. My supervisor recognizes my accomplishments.

1   **2**   **3**   **4**   **5**

11. I receive appropriate constructive criticism from my supervisor.

1   **2**   **3**   **4**   **5**

12. My supervisor involves me in important decisions relating to my job.

1   **2**   **3**   **4**   **5**

13. My supervisor responds to my suggestions.

1   **2**   **3**   **4**   **5**

14. My supervisor contributes to making my work fun.

1   **2**   **3**   **4**   **5**

15. My work is making a contribution to the success of the organization.

1   **2**   **3**   **4**   **5**

16. I like coming to work each day.

1   **2**   **3**   **4**   **5**

17. My assignments tap my strongest skills.

1   **2**   **3**   **4**   **5**

18. I am able to handle the administrative/paperwork part of my job.

1   **2**   **3**   **4**   **5**

19. I am making a difference with my work.

    1   **2**   **3**   **4**   **5**

20. The organization provides a quality product or service.

    1   **2**   **3**   **4**   **5**

21. I feel that upper management listens to my opinions.

    1   **2**   **3**   **4**   **5**

22. Our product or service is represented truthfully in the marketplace.

    1   **2**   **3**   **4**   **5**

23. My organization allows me to reach my full potential.

    1   **2**   **3**   **4**   **5**

24. The communication channels in my organization make it easy for me to get my job done.

    1   **2**   **3**   **4**   **5**

25. The executives in our organization show positive ways of interacting with other people in the organization.

    1   **2**   **3**   **4**   **5**

26. I see the organization fostering trust and collaboration.

    1   **2**   **3**   **4**   **5**

27. I see my personal values consistent with the values of the organization

    1   **2**   **3**   **4**   **5**

28. My organization contributes to the betterment of the community.

    1   **2**   **3**   **4**   **5**

TOTALS:

A quick total of your score will indicate where you stand.

Add the numbers up: _____

If your figures total from **112 to 140**, your results are *moderate* to *high*.

If your figures total from **84 to 112**, your results are *moderate*.

If your figures total **0 to 84**, your results are *moderate* to *low*.

YOUR TRANSITION JOURNAL

date _____

YOUR TRANSITION JOURNAL

date _____

YOUR TRANSITION JOURNAL

date _____

YOUR TRANSITION JOURNAL

date _____

YOUR TRANSITION JOURNAL

date _____

YOUR TRANSITION JOURNAL

date _____

ABOUT THE AUTHORS

Roy J. Blitzer, an Executive and Management Consultant, has over 23 years experience as a human resources and business management professional. He has held positions that ranged from Manager of Training and Corporate Communications at Roche Biosystems and Vice President at Achieve Global (formerly Zenger Miller) to Senior Consultant and Coach to firms in the Fortune 1000 and their senior staff.

Roy is certified and works with numerous assessment instruments and has a BA in English Literature from the University of Massachusetts at Amhurst and an MBA in Organizational Behavior from the University of California at Berkeley. He is an adjunct faculty member at the University of San Francisco, San Jose State University and Menlo College. His first book, Office Smarts: 252 Tips for Success in the Workplace, was published in 1994 and his articles have appeared in numerous journals and magazines. Roy produces and hosts his own television show, ASK "DR" BUSINESS.

Jacquie Reynolds-Rush, an executive and career management consultant, has 20 years experience in executive development, career consulting and human resource management.

She has been a Director of Training & Corporate Communications; a Divisional Vice President oif Executive Recruitment and Development and the Vice President of Human Resources for a large national retail company.

Jacquie has focused her efforts as a consultant in the area of career development.. She was a principal in Career Works, Inc. promoting career management through career development systems and products.